Arms and Legs and Other Limbs

By Allan Fowler

Consultants

Linda Cornwell, Learning Resource Consultant,
Indiana Department of Education

Sharyn Fenwick, Elementary Science/Math Specialist,
Gustavus Adolphus College, St. Peter, Minnesota

Janann V. Jenner, Ph.D.

Children's Press®
A Division of Grolier Publishing
New York   London   Hong Kong   Sydney
Danbury, Connecticut

Designer: Herman Adler Design Group

Library of Congress Cataloging-in-Publication Data

Fowler, Allan.
    Arms and legs and other limbs / by Allan Fowler.
      p. cm. – (Rookie read-about science)
    Includes index.
    Summary: Compares the two arms and two legs that humans have with
the limbs of other animals and how they are used.
    ISBN 0-516-20809-8 (lib. bdg.)   0-516-26478-8 (pbk.)
    1. Extremities (Anatomy)—Juvenile literature. [1. Anatomy, Comparative.
2. Extremities (Anatomy) 3. Arm. 4. Leg.] I. Titles. II. Series.
QM548.F68   1999   97-31278
591.47'9—dc21   CIP
                                       AC

What are your limbs?
How many do you have?

Your arms are limbs, and your legs are limbs. So you have four limbs. Many land animals have four limbs.

For many kinds of animals,
all four limbs are legs.

The two front limbs of monkeys and apes are arms with hands and fingers, much like yours.

Monkeys and apes use their arms and hands for eating, for cleaning each other's fur, and for swinging from branches. Even so, monkeys and apes usually walk on all four limbs.

Tassel–eared squirrel

Squirrels, raccoons, and otters are other animals that can grasp things with their front hands, or paws.

River otter

Some animals, such as kangaroos, have hind limbs that are much longer and stronger than their front ones. Their hind limbs are great for leaping!

Giraffes have the longest legs of any animal.

Harp seal

Legs and arms are not the only kind of limbs. Limbs can also be flippers, fins, or wings.

The limbs of a seal,
sea lion, or walrus
are flippers.

Pacific walrus

Birds have four limbs. Two of them are legs, and two are wings.

Some birds, such as these flamingos, have legs that bend backward instead of forward.

Don't try this yourself!

Ostriches run fast
on long legs.

Penguins waddle on short ones. Neither can fly, even though they have wings. A penguin uses its wings as oars when it swims.

The limbs of most fish are fins, which they use for swimming.

A few fish, such as the mudskipper, can use their front fins to walk on land, and even climb onto branches.

Insects have six legs.

Spiders have eight.

The eight limbs of an octopus are called tentacles.

Hawaiian lobster

Lobsters and crabs have ten limbs. Eight are legs for crawling, and two are claws for grasping things.

A centipede has dozens of legs.

Millipedes have even more than centipedes.

Imagine trying to walk with all those legs!

Centipede

Millipede

Agama lizard

Crocodiles, alligators, turtles, and most lizards have four legs.

Snakes have the least
number of limbs of
any animal—zero.

Four limbs seem right for us. Two legs for standing, walking, or running, one arm with a hand for holding this book . . .

. . . and another arm with
a hand to turn the pages.

Words You Know

claws

fins

flippers

limbs

paws

tentacles

wings

Index

About the Author

Allan Fowler is a freelance writer with a background in advertising. Born in New York, he now lives in Chicago and enjoys traveling.

Photo Credits

©: ENP Images: cover, 7 (Gerry Ellis); Photo Researchers: 19, 30 top right (Fletcher & Baylis), 3, 16, 17, 31 top left, 31 bottom right (Tim Davis), 21 (E.R. Degginger), 12 (Francois Gohier), 15 (M.P. Kahl), 25 bottom (L & D Klein), 25 top (Tom McHugh), 29 (P. Royer/Explorer), 27 (F. Stuart Westmorland), 23, 30 top left (Andrew G. Wood); Rigoberto Quinteros: 4, 5; Tom & Pat Leeson: 8, 31 top right; Visuals Unlimited: 10 (Walt Anderson), 22, 31 bottom left (Hal Beral), 20 (C.R. Calentine), 28 (Mark E. Gibson), 9, 11, 26 (Joe McDonald), 13, 30 bottom (Nada Pecnik).